THE WAY YOU KNOW IT

To Chrissie
with best wishes

THE WAY YOU KNOW IT

NEW & SELECTED POEMS

STUART HENSON

Stuart Henson

Shoestring Press

Printed by imprintdigital
Upton Pyne, Exeter
www.digital.imprint.co.uk

Typesetting and cover design by narrator
www.narrator.me.uk
info@narrator.me.uk
033 022 300 39

Published by Shoestring Press
19 Devonshire Avenue, Beeston, Nottingham, NG9 1BS
(0115) 925 1827
www.shoestringpress.co.uk

First published 2018
© Copyright: Stuart Henson

The moral right of the author has been asserted.

ISBN 978-1-912524-10-5

ACKNOWLEDGEMENTS

New Poems: *Agenda*; *Bare Fiction*; *Best British Poetry 2013* (Salt); *Ink, Sweat & Tears*; *Iota*; *London Magazine*; *London Grip*; *Magma*; *Modern Poetry in Translation*; *Poetry & All That Jazz* (Chichester Festival, 2018); *The North*; *Stand*; *Strike Up the Band* (Plas Gwyn Books, 2017); *The Dark Horse*; *The Interpreter's House*; *The Times Literary Supplement*; *The Spectator*; *The Warwick Review*.

'Sewing' was first published in *The Hudson Review* Vol LXIX No. 4, 2017

'The Shed' is one of *Ten Poems About Sheds* (Candlestick Press, 2018).

*

Selected Poems from: *The Impossible Jigsaw* (Peterloo Poets, 1985); *Ember Music* (Peterloo, 1994); *Clair de Lune*, with drawings by Mark Bennett, (Shoestring Press, 1998); *A Place Apart* (Shoestring, 2003); *The Odin Stone* (Shoestring, 2011); *Feast of Fools*, with illustrations by Bill Sanderson, (Shoestring, 2015).

'A Perspective of Mantegna' appeared in *The Spectator* in 1996 but is hitherto uncollected.

'Riddle' which was first published in 'The New Exeter Book' (1999) also appears in *The Heart's Granary, Poetry & Prose from Fifty Years of the Enitharmon Press* (2017).

'The Price' was reprinted in *100 Prized Poems: Twenty-five years of the Forward Books* (Forward Worldwide, 2016) and *The Poetry Pharmacy*, (Penguin/Particular, 2017).

for K.
and for John Greening
always my first readers

CONTENTS

VERSIONS

from *THE IMPOSSIBLE JIGSAW*

from *EMBER MUSIC*

from *CLAIR DE LUNE*

from *A PLACE APART*

New Poems

IT'S NOT WHAT YOU KNOW; IT'S THE WAY THAT YOU KNOW IT

like riding the back of the beat so sweetly
the whole band grooves there, deep in the pocket

or what it means when the swung trapeze
at the reach of its arc leans weightless

the moment you spring from the ledge—
or the blade's edge trusting the ice as you spin

or the heft of the wind and the thrust of the beach;
how the tied fly skips and the wet light leaps

or the bell tenor settles still on the stay or
the slave's released from his stone-bound sleep;

it's the brush on the sweep of the line cutting in,
the last pass of the mind as it aces the theorem.

The rest, as the man said, don't mean a thing
and it's not the tale; it's the slant telling.

FACELESS

I speak for the faceless
the sad without status
the folk who live under the hill
in a not-spot, a kind of hiatus;
whose profiles are lost
in a wasteland of lamp-fog
and books in odd places.

For the no-mates I sing
who are greyed, who are pale
as candles and blank as denial.
Unkindled, they fade
when you try to log-in—
like a Cheshire Cat's grin,
like the slightest of smiles.

ENTRANCE

And you, sweet soul, do you go by the lift or the stair?
When you click do your groceries come running
or do you wear out shoe-leather day by slow day
on the street between here and the discount store?

This building is forty mansions tall, with balconies
to the setting sun and a gated wall. When I asked
at the grille my voice sounded crumpled and way too small.
The CCTV had me covered: a chancer—a fraud.

My coat with no label was clearly unsuitable; it bore
all the hallmarks of ignorance. A youth with a beard
and his back to the dumpster sat nursing his Smirnoff.
He laughed that the code would be 1053 and he swore

Round the corner, he coughed, in the alleyway
east of the block, and he called it the poor door.

MARGINAL

The rumble of small sound-barriers
split in the skate-park
and everything tipped
on an arc of balance
all ready to pendulum down
to the hollow
where time runs away.

Cut grass, encoded with starlings,
a spray-fix of daisies.
The whine of the train's slung motors;
its bright singing line.
High cloud in the pond
where a moorhen constructs
her nest out of hamburger trays.

WINDOW-SHOPPING

The love of mannequins—purer than ours
in beauty unimpeachable, seamless of flesh,
milk-skinned, their taste immaculate
gaze long and haughty, cupid-blind.

Yet they have ghosts in place of mind:
misshapen creatures plunging past
who pause in poseless sequences to yearn
pug-ugly, wistful, flat as glass.

SEWING

So this is a story of silence, the sort of silence
you'd find in Vermeer or Burne-Jones, with a woman
sewing in light, in the windows' several reflections,
her hands chasing then still, like an animal in the world
beyond where a flicker of yellow leaves up and running
is animal too, where the trees are gathering cloud-race
and distance against the ends of a dying summer;
in the oak and the cherries, the small pale hands
of the maples whipped by the squall, in the unvoiced
swirl of the coming rain that threshes their tops
like anemones trawling an undertow—
as if all the strain of the hurrying air
were gathering there where the leaves are tricked
upward and out like stray souls in a rush for eternity
and the crab apples shake in the shape of a melody
as they fall now then and bounce to the place
where they'll rest and decay and be mined by the wasps
as her hands dip away and are lost in the roar
that you can't quite hear that is ever and everywhere.

SWEEPING

Each stroke a slight asthmatic swish
and where brush touches furniture
the cluck of chair leg, table, bench...
each hiccup at its proper pitch.

AFTER THE DANCE

for Margaret McMahon

He will come when the grasses
have given up their lights
and hogweeds darken against the sky.

He will come when the bats are plying
the arch of the copse
with their black, sporadic flight.

He will come when the woodbine
breathes its unbearable
sweetness adrift on the night

and long down the lane by the close
where the hedge-shadows drown
he will listen and wait.

He will fetch me home to the last barred gate
in the speechless dusk
as if it were not too late, too late.

THE HALL-STAND

Between the parlour and the stair
the mirror told you who you were:
black hat, black coat, gloves and umbrella,
the Hymnal and the Book of Common Prayer.

PHOTOGRAPHS OF MARY HILLIER

(in the studio of Julia Margaret Cameron 1864–1867)

I   Fruits of the Spirit

Temperance, Faith, Longsuffering, Meekness

I spy—a fly
crawling the back of the worn settee.

And still! she says. *Very still.*

In the camera I am wrong:
I am upside-down.

Indifference, Bitterness, Loneliness, Envy

That throng in the great obscure room of the future

what will they see?

II   Dark Room

Time puddles. The plate gives up
its muddy secrets.

A child still. Very still.

If I am still and I squint
then the world will be…

glazed with the faintest craquelure.

Her thumb.

And Goodness, Love, Gentleness, Peace…

III   Joy

I cannot lie
says the pearly eye.
Imagine, says she

(This is serious)

the joy in her the womb as the Spirit flies.

O the giving up!

(She unclasps my hands)

O the ecstasy!

IV   A Song

And sweet Kate Dore has taken the place
in the picture where I should be.
Her forehead is bright and her soul is clear
not puzzled by shadows like me.

V   Call and I Follow

Unmasked at last. My stupid heart.

A garret where the dusk caught fire.
Morning and night. Not quite Elaine.
Not quite pre-Raphaelite.

Slow lidded eyes; lip's overbite
Head turned on black—barge cloth
and the folds of my wild hair's tragedy.

Life chases art. Morning and night.

These soap-scoured hands.

Cracked glass. White sands.

Time's river back to Astolat.

VICTORIAS

Old gnarl of a tree that grew out through the shed wall
wedged inbetween its boards and the brick of the shared privy.
No doubt it was there before they were built:
its knots, its dust, the snails themselves, were Victorian.

You could scale a limb, lean out where fence and sky
split the world in two—for the weight of their gold, the prize
of their shape, for their skins silked like a tawny breast—
and their pocks of brown lace that the wasps had etched.

RILKE IN A CONVENT GARDEN

Roses in a south wind, threshing at the storm's door.
No answer. The thunder sliding its bolts.
Spun cloud, possessed with its boiling of violence;
and the roses' unrest, their desire, their distress.

Then the morning, treacherous with jasmine,
the air of the cloister so thick that the bells on the rooftop
will drip their cracked drops through its heaviness—
through the pond of breathed incense released in its depths.

HEN PARTY IN THE BORGO PINTI

Sometimes the old gods riot in the streets:
they want their dues, their rites, their bacchanal.
Priapus leers. Diana turns, appalled.
Her maids mutate to gorgons on his sweets
high like these tipsy acolytes complete
with all the trimmings on their tottering heels
who mock her bridal with a cake and veil—
one last anarchic licence of release.

When carnival held hands with poverty
their dance was orgiastic, drum-bound, wild:
no grace next day to undo what was done.
Tomorrow's morning-after of fertility
will wake coiled in her tutu, vomit-spoiled,
that big pink sugar cock sucked to oblivion.

ROTONDA

Giardino della Montagnola, Bologna

There are models of time that run straight
and some that are skeined in a figure of eight
and others that swallow their tails like snakes
condemned to consume themselves on a ring.

And the slow old man in the dust of the park
intent on unwinding the knots of his chain
who shuffles around and again and again with his unbroken step
like the minute hand of some ancient clock.

Here today and then yesterday and the day
before that, it's his task, or his exercise, his way
of recovering what escapes at his back
where the trees breathe out light and the high clouds skim

and the sky's blown with cracks in a pattern
of twigs that bud open and puzzle the sun.

ON TAKING MY FATHER'S *KEATS* TO ROME

Not passport sized, and bound in worn green hide:
a Kingsgate Pocket Poets at half-a-crown.
'To My Dearest Brother' from his sister Joan
inscribed for his birthday, 1945—
when he was Keats's age but glad to be alive
entrained in France and headed for Cologne.
In '44 he didn't get to Rome,
shipped back through Naples lucky to survive.

Now this frail keepsake leads me to the grave
of one for whom the Italian sun was meant
to warm the blood, to seal his lungs' dark scars.
What heals the mind? (Poor Severn couldn't save
his friend) Time's distances? A book's small print?
Mute patience grieving like that last late star?

A DANCER ON THE SPANISH STEPS

What catches the eye is her stillness— a *Little Danseuse*
on the sunlit terrace, poised, like a leaf about to fall.

She's all done out in leotard and tulle and ballet shoes.
Street art? No, photographs. Her mother as a Degas chaperone.

Repeat. Repeat each pose. Alonge and petit battement and skip
into the next, each balustrade her bar, her zoetrope.

And this: light stretched on stone, split persimmons—
their jellied gape, green chatter of Rome's parakeets…

Such things in cities where, to strangers, no-one's known
and small feet trip; cage-birds speak babel, flying free.

LIBRAIRIE

Today a muse is playing games with me.
She follows in the shadows till I slip
out of the autumn sun into the bookshop
on the *Rue de la Parchminerie*.
And there she disappears beguilingly
among the shelves: I think I see her grip
a stack and bend and pull and squeeze her hips
into the section labelled *Poetry*.

A room, a secret space, hidden behind
the edifice of language by absurd
co-incidence or irony, where she
the priestess of its sesame design
is free to come and go, to re-emerge
offering alternatives—or tea, or coffee.

THE MEASUREMENT OF TIME ON THE CALLE REVERENDO PONS

At noon, the steep street is shadowless
and straight as a gnomon, the sky
a blue slip in the gap between eaves.

While you sleep off the heat,
in his workshop the artist Paco completes
a thousand scales for a carnival float.

And at two on the slope above him
Manolo moves on with his goats
under olives old as the terraces.

By three the tin chime of their bells
will be threaded behind
the cleft of the hill.

Then at half past four the widow Inés
will open the doors of her pigeon-house
so the white birds revolve

where the rooftops give way
to a mountain storm: slow-purple,
the violet of columbine

LETATLIN
or *The Workers' Flying Bicycle*

being notes toward the production of a human flying machine—
Vladimir Tatlin, 1929

1

Updraft of birds
their soft velocities
whose bones are flute notes—no
are piccolo. I puzzle this
and gravity, and Leonardo's
lines—their flow.

2

A cliff thermal—
and a red hawk riding its spiral
steep on the flexing air...
So Icarus, sweet youth and tall
the sun's laughter; the wax tears
weeping his fall.

3

One whore they called
the village bicycle I knew:
fickle as March, her eyes sky-blue.
We pedalled quick, we stalled
we gasped aloft
freewheeled—and flew.

4

Her corset, cast,
a canvas wing.
Trussed strings unlaced;
pale corrugated waist un-clasped.
That crimp, that hunger-tight embrace.
Its grasp.

5

Bright beaks in the cherries.
Some wild belief
when the skylark sings
and the larches creak
that spring's not a week away—
on a green wind.

6

A dragonfly—with its raindrop eye
and its meshes, its dapples,
its blue electricity. Tripped spark
fizzed polarities—
and its one slight volt
arced to earth on my knee.

7

Your measure—a man.
Four cubits. His hands spread
at the circle's span. Chest's rise
and chest's fall, all his breathless desire...
The blood and steel wire
of creation's plan.

A COSY CRIME

('Cosy Crime'—a classification at Waterstones bookshop, Leeds)

The body, sagged in the armchair, drooling slightly.
Her upturned teacup's left a large, unsightly

stain the shape of Africa in the lap of her dress.
No sign of violence, nothing disturbed, no mess

except the patch of something sticky on the pantry
floor: that and the sunlight's late forced entry.

Across the road behind the nets at number thirty-eight
the Cartwrights play sudoku in the advert break:

Toyota Avensis: Sponsor of ITV Mystery Drama.
'We can't believe that anyone could want to harm her...'

Tonight they'll watch the news and see themselves,
seated in front of all the green spines on their shelves.

There is the son, of course, but he was sixty miles away
engaged in Mortal Combat with a friend—he says.

The milkman and the girl who brings the Meals on Wheels;
the once-a-fortnight handyman who cuts the hedge and steals

a tenner from her purse while she's still looking for the biscuit
tin (old dear's so blind he thinks this once he'll risk it);

the agent in the suit who wanted her to sell, release the equity:
you check them one by one for motive, opportunity.

Fine comb the carpet. Crumbs but no clues.
Your job's to add it up, make sense, put two and two

together, weigh the facts you've got to build a case on.
That's all the evidence. Now make your accusation.

THE LARSEN TRAP

Your magpie flaps and hops,
his wire box
no bigger than a rabbit hutch.
The rabbit—guts,
flesh, eyes—supplies
the prisoner's last meal, whose cries
lure and incriminate
its next inmate.

No keeper rhymed these birds with joy.
Two for a death. One for a decoy.

FUGIT AMOR

Love is always tumbling into the past
becoming then instead of now
so quickly it could break your heart.

At least you say catch me a photograph
to save the day as if a click somehow
could stop it tumbling to the past.

But time is fleet and far too smart
to fall for that old trick and not allow
your love to slip and break your heart.

Despair the solaces of art:
brush, ink and manuscript have practised how
to show love tumbling to the past.

And if you didn't cry you'd laugh
at those who fight, refuse to let love go,
for even so it breaks their hearts.

Is it too much to hope, to ask
a moment to forget, just not to know
that love is always tumbling into the past
so quickly it will numb then break your heart?

THE SHED

Step in it's a tardis: vortex of smells
distilled a century—of pre-war
timber, earth-floor, and the gold decay
of sawdust, linseed, two-stroke oil.

Is this what happens, then? All falls
in place as you're sucked down
through boards and beams, the sun's migraine
toward some backward ebb of space

by webs of rope-slack, amber panes
that seem to stain long afternoons
left there alone, lost to make sense
of time's great centrifuge, its huge mistake.

Now while you shrink to half your size
bemused by beetle-sift, hammocks of flies
you marvel at the fat bench vice
haunched like a Buddha on its height—

that and the square-tanked Velocette
you scramble on and don scuffed
gauntlets, goggles, Biggles-eyed,
throat-rev the throttle, ease the brake.

Behind, dry wallflowers and trellises,
tall shadows reaching to embrace…
Kick down my canny lad. Accelerate.
Back to the future and its great escape.

AFTER THE EQUINOX

The tractor's grind and the gulls' white screech.
The plough still drawing its steady lines on the earth's skin.

And each clod rolled like a tired old dog
who just wants to sleep in the last of the sun.

INTERLUDE

It must be dusk—that interlude
when day breathes out and all that's left's
a trail of gulls rippling the emptiness,
when everything approximates to music in the heart:
a vapour-scrawl high on the blue,
the moon a watermark...
Weltschmerz, a desperate accidie
to which all sorrow tends, all good.

And twelve balloons set out at intervals
across the sunset like some great tone-row.
Largo of solitude, each almost motionless
adrift toward the evening's edge,
their sudden tacit fire-tails
lifting across the darkness of a wood.

INK CAPS

October: wet earth and a nightmare of tat in the shops.
Where there used to be shouting, flung sticks
and the conkers drying like clots in the grass
they arrive in their crowds in their boats of decay
to jostle, to clown where the buried stump rots—
in the graveyard—a fine place as any for ghosts
to come shouldering up from their underworld
in flayed bonnets pyjamas and smut-deckled smocks

and they seem to be waiting, like question marks
that stand mute and expectant and oddly bemused
or like children who knock at the door in the dark.
They're unfazed by confusion. What sets them apart
is their patience their anger their slow fade to black
when we don't understand what it is that they ask.

ATTACHMENT

Through the little window of the photograph
you smile back: three hundred miles north,
three thousand feet above Ben Lomond's loch
where the wind flatters your cheekbones,
your shoulders nudge the peaks apart.

Old paths are drifting under snow;
the modem reaches out to wirelessness.
Two metres all the rope we have from screen to this:
your scarf tugged at the air's quick wish,
a sky grown heavy with its promises.

POSTCARD FROM ALDEBURGH

to JG

Sheer salt-bright light and a long shingle shore.
It drags your steps back as if the stones' pull
could sprawl you down and under like the rolled
grey waves that swell, smack, tumble and withdraw.
A place where not much grips: one pink crab claw,
seablite, horned poppies' blasted tentacles;
the fingers of a hundred shipwrecked souls
that cried out mercy in the breakers' roar.

Is it them you can hear in the backwash—
the pebbles chattering against the foam?
Raise up a shell and listen for that sound:
the wind, or Grimes' apprentices, the lost
girls huddled in the hulk *Ionia*...
high crowding voices that will not be drowned.

LOST MUSIC

for John Lucas and for the trio that played in Yates's

Three hours a night, and twice a week
not counting impros and repeats
that's half a million notes a year
or twenty thousand speckled sheets
of classics lite, decades of parts
bagged in some landfill's mouldering dark.

Pearl Fishers, Stardust, Lara's Theme...
Play them again! Lost melodies
tunes gone like names of friends
met way back when, on Yates's balcony—
songs redolent with moth-ball scents,
a fiddle's threadbare eloquence.

Moonlight Serenade, The Lambeth Walk...
Snug by the mirrors there we're caught
in Manet poses, sipping port
and smoke, while down below old soaks
in brogues and tweeds, collars and ties
grow ruddy cheeked and sad and wise.

Outside it's cold. The last bus waits.
Don't fold that page. Don't shut the lid.
Don't slide that sax back in its case!
Ply just once more—for old times' sake
Blue Danube, None but the Lonely Heart...
the tram-wire staves, those time-foxed charts.

INTERVALS OF VEILED GLARE

*...when the sun broke through gave me a pain in the heart
and a hang in the head.*

Eric Ravilious: letter to Edward Bawden, 16th Sept 1937

salt air unfocused brightness so intense
your cheekbones wince whole face
clenched tight against that bleached immensity

white flare slab bulk of ships that sink
like quays against the weight of grey
shifting like continents

sometimes they up and slip their horizontals
meek as dreams tide-runnels fritter sly gulls screech
lugworms excrete their sand meringues

go home young man take tea make love
sea is a nerveless thing latent and deep
vast as eternity and wide as sleep

FIELDFARES

a Viking raid
at the wood's edge

with their grey hoods
and blood on their vests

they laugh as they pillage
the blackbird's kist:

on the bones of the hedge
not a red drop left

BUZZARD AS CAESAR

Sloe-blue: a ripening darkness
pressed on the skyline—
horizon hauling the iron down
in the storm's interval

and the stubbles drying, paler than sand

Then the buzzard's cere
in the sudden sun
dipping as the wind tips him

Imperial casting—atop the trees' march

so he's high on the din of advance
all the clouds' legions massed
and magnificent

with the light split in his eye like a prism
like Arcus

her righteous curved sword

WAIT

(Henry Williamson, Stiffkey, Norfolk, 1938)

Out of the dark they speak, voices like owls',
the poets calling each to each again,
distinct yet coded: Thomas through the rain's
mesh, something akin to the wind howling
across the salt marsh, strangulated vowels
scarcely distinguishable though he strains
to separate the truth, the praise, the pain,
from nature's chaos where his last hope drowns.

Fasces and Eagles and the ruse of peace;
the politics too little and too late…
He lies all night beside his shotgun, wild-eyed,
begging old comrades for a quick release.
And death holds out the hand he once denied
until one cries from woods near Arras, *Wait!*

SAVINGS

All this the hedgerow saves
from the underworld:

a wire of blood-drops
necklace of blisters

and the dots of crabs
pressed on the sky in yellow braille

or stashed under leafmould
the blackbird's counting-book

the odd dark sloe
dried like a raisin

that and the rain's
midwinter silver

too soon spent
on buying back the sun

Versions

THE WATER NYMPH

(Alexandr Pushkin)

Alone, where the lake laps at the root
of ancient alders, peat-steeped oaks,
the anchorite, praying, starving, praising,
scoops out his own grave, pausing
at last to look right through the sunset
to the throne of God, his heart molten,
his soul infatuated now with holy fear.

Meanwhile the black horizon seems
to suck all daylight from the cloud,
the wood silts up and the moon
draped only in her blooded rags
draws vapours from the lake-top
like a mist of mayflies rising
and boiling on the brooding air.

Then, as he gazes on the mirror-face,
the drowned sky shudders and his sweat
dries cold. Out of the hidden moil
a girl shines upward from the depth, slipping
weed silks from shoulder, breast, hip...
turning to lie, hair spread and legs astride
the rock that outcrops on the farther shore.

Her stare is deeper than desire: it says
swim to me if you dare; I am the pool,
the spawning-place. Give up. Confess
and I'll absolve your body's torture.
And when he groans she knows and smiles
and plunges back into the water,
silver and instant as a shooting-star.

Prayer is a lost cause. All the next day
his spirit whores among a hundred

shifting images of her. Will she be there
when the moon crawls slowly
from the sagging shades and shapes
that congregate at dusk beyond the lake
to watch him watching from his door?

And yes, she comes and mocks him
once and one night more, flaunting
her ferny loins and splashing, calling
the monk with pouts and tearful eyes
and little chastely breathless sighs,
only to dive and leave him sunk and shaken,
haunted by the pretty trickle of her laughter.

Three nights; two lead-weight dawns.
The fourth morning ash-wraiths
skitter from his fire and the monk's door keens
on its hinge. Nikolai and Dimitri, fishing,
hook in the mealed corpse, the tangled beard,
the sackcloth rolling where the currents
swell across the lake's uneven floor.

AFTER PUSHKIN

Caught in the clatter of a city street,
or stepping through the still hush of a church,
or at a gig, maybe, crushed in the mosh-pit,
my mind plays God, reminding me that each

of us must pass into the world of darkness
when the years run down his little store of light.
Among the hundreds there who push and press
one may be due to stage-dive out tonight.

Look at that oak. My father climbed that tree's
green limbs, and so did I; yet every spring
when I'm gone it will delete those memories
and burn a brand new summer in its rings.

Even to hold a baby is to take
the time-bomb of the future in your hands.
He sleeps now, all potential. When he wakes
his expectations detonate my end.

Each day I turn the diary's page—another
week, another month, a year—I try to guess
which is my last; when will the calendar
mark nothing but the blank space of my death.

And sometimes, too, I stop and wonder *where?*
Out on a lake, caught by a freakish wave?
Maybe the innocent victim of a war
I didn't make, flung in a hasty grave?

My corpse won't care. But still, let it be near
the places that I learned to love—one
corner of some local field; a space where kids
make out, and new shoots break, warmed by the sun.

ARION

(Alexandr Puskkin)

The decks were swarmed with mariners:
slaves hauling the sheets in,
boys crawling like spiders in the rigging,
the power-house plunging the great oars
in the foam, and calm in that storm
of action our silent helmsman, setting course
for home on a dead-reckoning.
And me, naturally, with my art, my poetry,
my happy heart, my off-key singing...
Before the tornado tore us apart.
Survivors? You must be joking!
Oarsman, hands, helmsman, lost to a man.
No-one but me, ringing out my soaking shirt,
humming a line from a new verse,
unhurt, with my bum in the sun-dried sand.

MIDNIGHT MASS

after the prose-poem 'Le Messe de Minuit' by Aloysius Bertrand

Christus natus est nobis; venite, adoremus

'We have neither hearth nor home
Though we pray God's will be done'

In the vaulted hall of Chateauvieux the chaplain was saying the grace. Her Ladyship takes bread in her hands—but wait. The clicking of youthful feet at the door, their clogs, and the plaintive chant of a carol.

'My Lady of Chateauvieux, make haste, for everyone's beating a path to the church and the candle that burns at your prie-dieu in the chapel of angels is dripping its little wax stars on your book of hours, on your velvet cushion. Make haste lest it breathe its last!' That's what rang out in the first peal of the bells for midnight mass.

'My noble Lord of Chateauvieux, the Earl of Grugel is passing below, his lantern ablaze. Make haste or he'll take your place of honour among the good souls of the Grocers' Guild.' Thus spake the second peal of the bells for midnight mass.

'Good Father the Chaplain, brook no delay. The organ is rolling its terrible bass, the choir's in process, the faithful are gathered to make their peace while you sit elbows at rest on the board.' The voice of the third peal of the bells for midnight mass.

And so at the gothic porch with its dusting of snow the children, blowing their fingers warm, were not to wait long for their sweets and a sixpence given to each by the priest in his patrons' name.

*

Meanwhile, as the bells were rung down, Her Ladyship, neck-deep in her furs, and His Lordship, sporting his Justice's hood, set out, and the Chaplain shuffled along in pursuit—in his clerical cloak with his missal tucked under his arm.

47

THE BUILDER

after the prose-poem 'Le Maçon' by Aloysius Bertrand

Way up there where he's treading the scaffolded air, drill in hand, a spirit of the great gold dome's reflections, Ahmed Nasib stands astride with his feet on a skyline of block-work and spires, its thirty sharp minarets—the horizon's finials.

He's singing along to a song in his ear while the adhan flares from the mouths of the tower to the street-void below, to the cliff falls of concrete and glass and the shell-gape that nestles the slant of a kestrel's motionless wing...

While he watches the fort, with its pastry-cut walls crimped like a star; the compound; the hospital; the checkpoint... And even so distant the guards with their helmets, their lip-mics and aerials, the bulk of their blast-flaps, their body armour.

In sunlight the screen of a humvee winks back, and slowly the shadows are turning about the mast on the landing-strip and the look-out post and the squat white bricks of the peace-keepers' four-by-fours.

And there's more: in the stadium where the dust whips up into miniature ghosts that hurry a moment then stumble, exhale, Ahmed Nasib observes through the heat the police popping a shy of tin cans from one pockmarked crossbar.

Till at last in the dusk when the broad mosaic floor of the mosque is rolled up into shade, he looks out from his ladder across to the village far off—a comet against the blue of the night where the houses are burning, the rockets still fall.

NIGHT-HAWKS

after the prose-poem 'Les Gueux de Nuit 'by Aloysius Bertrand

'Froze my bones and froze my heart,
How long this cold it gonna last?'

'Hey! Shift and let's get near the fire. You're all over it like you're shagging it! And this poor wanker's skinny as a cocktail-stick.

'One a.m. A draught from hell. D'ya know why the moon's so bright then, Owly-eyes? They're burning bankers' bonuses.

'But hell's red as these embers, with blue flames like paraffin. And, hey, which one of you's the bastard smackin' up his bitch?

'My prick's an icicle!' 'Balls roasting like chestnuts.' 'Whatya see in the fire, Dog-boy?' 'Flick-knives.' 'N' you, Rasta?' 'An eye.'

Look up! The Secretary for Social Services all kitted out in thermals and fur hat. Her nipples won't be freezing off.

The polis too. 'Catch up with that click didya?' 'We tazered one. He had a gun. The others legged it quick across the bridge.'

*

That's how the MP slumming the soup-run and her po-faced officers got cosy with us bums around the brazier. Before they pissed off home to file reports or tell their story down the nick.

MOONLIGHT

after the prose-poem 'Le Clair de Lune' by Aloysius Bertrand

Ah, sweetness—with Big Ben's midnight chime still echoing—
to gaze at the moon shining like a new pound coin!

*

A chorus: two drunks under my window and a dog chained in the
next-door yard.

And then a silence so profound you can hear the tick of the
traffic-lights and streets away the ghost of a scream.

Now the dog's curled down on his rusting links, lulled by a siren,
a distant train.

The traffic-lights still cycle their messages—in red, amber,
turquoise—their semaphore from the depths of space.

And the moon—it seems to me as the drug kicks in—is a face
begging its executioner. A victim in some asymmetric war.

from *The Impossible Jigsaw*

POACHER IN JANUARY

A south-west wind and mild enough for spring.
Bush elder irritates its purple buds,
in each a twitch, a chrysalis of wings.
The rain has pasted down and spread the clods
and spattered up a gritty wash of starlings
that wheel and furl a hushed smoke. The game birds
wait, loaded in the hedge like clays. He swings
the car door shut. One rapid pigeon whirrs.

The wind deflects his shadow as it strikes
across the flooded ruts and the oblique
slant of day stipples fools' gold in their tin.
Sunk silhouette, he crouches in the dyke:
the water-alloy strip conducts the sun—
blue barrel tilts; light earths along his gun.

GOING HOME

Forty years on he found a book that eulogised
the view of Naples from the sea. The way they
had arrived on broken roads, picking their track
among discarded armour, mines, was not to catch
the mist of pinks, campanulas, the biscuit walls
and garden hills from Castellammare to Sorrento.

All he recalled was they were going home, that
and the mess of tiny rowing-boats that crawled
about the troopships in the bay: so many hungry
and so many poor—their fruits and sweetmeats
hoisted up on ropes, the coins and notes let down,
dumb-waitered from the decks in packing-trays.

Vesuvius had growled a month before and still
its sky was heavy with the dust that bathed
an early sunset on the quay—flame in those
towers where the glass remained. Hot terraces
had cooled, and black against the gold-leaf wake
gulls cried to test the silence of the guns.

*

The train pulled out of Liverpool at eight
and not a thought was shared except a sense
of anti-climax: docked with the tide in a false
dawn, eleven days aboard the boat, somebody heard
the regimental band and then the carriages drew in,
smoky and warm, patterned with dust of past rain.

A change at Crewe and time to shave, surprised
by stranger's eyes and the burnt cheekbones.
Revival with the bitter tea, and all the rest
sat up and wondering at huge green elms, slate
yards and grass in parks, the aimless lanes
choking their gates with cow-parsley and may.

And lulled against the rhythm of the sway
unconsciously the mind rehearsed, as nets of thicket
shaped their sequences, the gate latch clack
the cinder path, a shadow moving in the room
and by the known backdoor a trellis fence
where old earth-scented lilies breathed their pain.

A SIMPLE GAME

Beyond the glass it is all quite silent:
the tall bossed spires of the hollyhocks,
the stones of the bird-bath brimming with light
and the boy counting at hide-and-seek
who will lose the purpose he runs to find.

Inside at the shutter a man is curled
like a snail-shell with his arms round his knees,
and veiled by the lint of dust
and the trees' melting against the panes
he too is lost in the sweep of time.

Till the child runs in and the room
with its own warmth of the autumn sun
is disturbed by the rap of his feet on the boards.
At each nook of the furniture footsteps stop.
he is not sure he should be here alone.

So he pulls a face in the pendulum clock
and lifts the web on the musical jug;
and discovers the book of Kipling
still with the same damp lumber-smell
and a rose of mould where his fingers are.

As the child reads and the mongoose leaps
the man has uncurled himself from his place
for he knows now he will not be seen:
though his lips move he can speak no word
and the floor is the falling floor of dream.

THE BOARDING HOUSES

O voi che siete in piccioletta barca...

Such villas bleach their arc along the strand
of any small resort where spume and sand
drew principled Victorians to dare
a white improper leg or take the air,
and somehow still these réchauffé hotels
preserve within their pastel walls the smells
of time, a jealous faded dignity,
an aura of restraint and sympathy.
A peacock stuffed and cased moth-eyes the stair;
the plastic flowers are arranged with care.
'Our guests, our regulars, come back each year,
though some will not return next time I fear.
Some of them say they used to go abroad.'
The seasons' grains trickle between the boards.
Behind the formal lace breakfast at nine
while on the beach the ski-girls wetsuits shine.
Age is the irritant, the pearl desire.
The gulls wheel in the sun, spiral and gyre.
From every room a view of ships that hide
behind the false horizon's rim; the tide
lifts half-hour trippers nimble round the head.
The glare is pitted in a sea like lead.

A STRANGE SECRET VIRTUE

(Virginia Ferrar)

Her palm coved like a spoon—
a handful of silk-seed
four score of grains
warming against her skin's heat.

They will hatch soon—
an open drawer
and her heart budding
wise as the mulberry.
Crab-apple, poplar, oak, cherry…
a green secret:
each sheathed bud
each single shoot
as it folds out its cramp
is speaking a part of it.

Wisdom—the pure silk word!
And these motes
on the arteries of leaf,
a crawling braille.
Sleeping, eating as one
they grow through their moults
as a class might grow
through the grades of school.

Six weeks—a girl's eyes
in the span of two moons:
the great white worms
are swaying, swaying
to find their perch.
Like a tale of elves
they will spin and spin.
For their eight more days
they will treadle skeins—

to their holocaust
in a pot of lye.

In this proficiency
she has taught herself.
For the cycle's wealth
she will keep the best
of the last cocoons.
As they tunnel out
the flake-grey flies
are falling about the room
like ash.

On the line
of that same white palm
they stir and couple.
The male she blows aside
in a quick flittering;
the female, shrouded
for pregnancy, is stowed away
in a linen womb.

When the girl looks up
from the wings of her moths,
she has heard
in the dusk of trees
the late bell
calling the house
to prayer.

Her God is reeling her into his hands
on the fine unbroken thread
of her life,
by a bidding skill
by the sleight of each turn.

from *Ember Music*

THE MUSIC OF WATER

In the beginning this was the first sound:
after the rush of chaos, sudden calm,
the stones in their places, waiting, the warm
light splashing and dappling shapes on the ground.
Then issues from the womb of time a drowned
boy surfacing: the first and naked Adam,
his lips gummed, his tongue thick, grunting a psalm
to Earth that aches about him like a wound.

Until he stops and cocks his ear to listen.
A stream, trickling and talking to his thirst
and teaching him to speak in words that glisten,
turn, drop, like water as it swells and bursts
on a thorn in the sun. And he is risen
now, a man. Ready to fall and be cursed.

THE PLAYERS

Out of the green graves or the road's dust
the dusk assembles them, wisest and least
like shadows gathered to a feast,
and one by one in candle-fall they come
about the chestnuts and the tombs,
speaking their dumb discourse to leaf
to stone and to the sun that lingers
low on the hill where the hay lies mown.

Gargoyles that once were angels hang and grin.
Above the sunken lane the dead lean in.
All the quick world is spring and listening
at time's conventicle, a ring
where thin grey fingers pluck at strings
that resonate through bird-light,
bat-light, half-light, out on the air
on the dim concentric circles of the night.

Their text, their eloquence, begins to be
our understanding too and our intelligence
is rhymed to theirs and hears as if the trees
translated us; but what they say's grown
brown with lichens, rain-washed, worn away.
Their day has travelled with its dusty sun
and goes ahead, and if we follow them we know
we should become them finally and not return.

For once these players might have been
priest, poet, teacher, physician...
But now the leather on their heels
is wearing thin. Their eyes see through us
and they're gone, beyond our hearing,
down the drift road where time and timeless join,
turning their pocket-silver twice for luck,
for a moon like the edge of a new coin.

THE PRICE

Sometimes it catches when the fumes rise up
among the throbbing lights of cars, or as
you look away to dodge eye-contact with
your own reflection in the carriage-glass;
or in a waiting-room a face reminds you
that the colour supplements have lied
and some have pleasure and some pay the price.
Then all the small securities you built
about your house, your desk, your calendar
are blown like straws; and momentarily,
as if a scent of ivy or the earth
had opened up a childhood door, you pause,
to take the measure of what might have been
against the kind of life you settled for.

LATE TRAIN

These carriages have plied their trade all day
in the to-fro heat from King's Cross up to
Peterborough; minute by airless minute
in their net of steel and high wire: the shimmer
on the parallel, throb of the power car—
continuous shrinking to a vanishing-point,
an always-coming, always-getting-there.
And now in the cool night, the vents open
and sucking in the still-warm smells, oily
unwholesome and evocative, they reel
once more, and I leaf through a book, recall
a man in winter clothes waist-deep in grass
who gathered lupins in the wilderness
between the slow-line and the dead canal;
the house-backs and the businesses, the yards;
the curious legend 'May Be Tamped' in rough
block letters on a bridge; and the number
CHAncery 8800, the ghost-phone
of an office-cleaning company, preserved
above graffiti-reach on a warehouse wall.
Now, in the late train, no-one needs to talk
and at the stops no voice disturbs or shouts
until the sudden bleeping of the doors
announces motion and restores the pulse
that nods these journey-makers on the breast
of sleep and soothes their day-won statuses.
The woman opposite is fair, full-limbed
and of an age that's done with innocence.
About my age. But still that unselfconscious
rag-doll falling of her head's pure childhood.
Sleep takes us like a mother to her trust.
And as my thought goes straggling at that edge
I dream of Patsy Toesland and Rosemary
and Cheryl Dant: the girls who held my hand
on the first day of school in the big land
beyond the garden of my first five years,

66

or naturally were generous and teased
me with a smile or the promise of a kiss.

The late train rocks these random passengers
till they become all whom I have forgotten
but knew once. Souls journeying by chance,
I muse how you might be asleep somewhere
like this and travelling the spinning night
on other trains to other towns and yet
all drawn down lines of time's discovered map
darkly towards some island of the blessed.

GIRL WITH A CAT

(after the painting by Pierre-Auguste Renoir, 1880)

It is morning in the Rue Cortot,
warm morning; the sunlight crumbles the walls
like bread and the dust falls
in the window's eye and delights
with its touch the surface of things.
There are bees in the garden,
the dew is gone. A grey dappled cat
lies asleep in a quoin of the roof
and below in the courtyard
an old woman sings.

Angèle, how you prattle—of nothing,
of lives, of the warmth of the sun,
but you can't sit still
and your dark lids droop
and the picture that Monsieur Renoir
has begun is nothing—no good.
You are young; you must sleep
you have love on your side
and your pert young face is your fortune
though not for long.

In the courtyard the woman is feeding the cat;
it curls round her feet with its fur
like smoke. It purrs and it arches
and dips at the milk. The painter leans out
with his hands on the sill. The garden
is full of the light of poppies and daisies,
shade-alleys of grasses and speechless leaves…
but the frame of the window
is suddenly empty—Renoir is descending
the staircase in leaps.

She is young; she must sleep;
her heart's hopes are simple; her face is her fortune
though not for long. And Monsieur Renoir
has begun again in his *grande affaire*
with the surface of things.
It is morning in the Rue Cortot,
warm morning; from the courtyard below
the smell of bread baking.
The cat shuts its eyes in the street-girl's lap
and the painter smiles and his brushes sing.

THE LOST BOYS

(Studio photograph, 1898)

'Those frank eyes where deep I see
An angelic gravity…'

At two years old your sister is too young
to invent the future: she sits intent,
absorbed in some small thinking of her own.
But you, in button-waisted Norfolk suits,
breeches, sharp new white collars, handkerchiefs,
what griefs beyond the camera's eye begin
to cloud gazes like yours? Is that the cause,
the portrait photograph lodged at your feet—
of your brother, Clement, dead aged seven,
haunting you then as it might haunt us now,
lost behind glass, wistful and far-away
though safe enough from all but sunlight's slow
decay? Is it the camera's black pall?
Or maybe in the lens's kaleidoscope
you see the tumbling century ahead
fall and reshape itself into a war
whose odds will take one of the three of you:
Rupert, who drew, was fine and sensitive
and married young; Wilfrid, astute, canny,
quick to make fun of art and bookishness;
or Julian whose studies took him on
to university and schoolteaching—
Arnold and Tennyson, the pregnant lines
For we are all, like swimmers in the sea,
Poised on the top of a huge wave of fate,
Which hangs uncertain to which side to fall.
Well, fate's wave, duly, as you knew it would,
crashed and went sprawling up the beach of time
and left the image of the moment there
when you were posed together in the frame
knowing somehow that this was serious,

that childhood was a grave and separate thing,
solemn like church, profound, soon to be gone.
Outside the studio the afternoon
was bright and sharp, and the shops were open.
The horse-drawn trams were rattling down the street.
Somebody in an office by the docks
was totalling a ledger; someone else
was checking with the harbour-master's clock
to make sure that his boat would catch the tide.
The world. Pride and responsibility.
And destiny, which you stepped out to meet.

EMBER MUSIC

The raked-out coals are glowing in the hearth,
crisp, cokey, light they jingle on the grate
like tiny chimes blown by their own last heat.
The chimney draws their music up; its breath
excites them into flower—flame-petal wreath
to all of day that's fallen through and spent.
The rest is ash, no more than ash; once burnt
it says each nightfall is a kind of death.

We crouch to warm our hands against the mesh
and listen for the tin-foil threnody.
You call it sleigh-bells distant over ice,
I think of spheres: the way the world turns once
from dawn to darkness in a day; the rest
is ash, no more than ash, and powdery.

ELEGY FOR AN OLD CARPET

When they began to cut them into shapes
of rooms, carpets stopped travelling.
New carpets spread unblemished over cracks
and gaps, and bland as chat-show hosts
declare: This Is Your Future. Start Again.
The old ones coil their secrets, stains
and dark mottlings, pock-marks of chairs.
They hoard their spillages, and those
unfaded squares of time trapped under furniture,
and doggedly they still refuse to turn
to hide the paths our daily footsteps wear.

I shall be sorry when this one has gone,
the Wilton from an ancient aunt
we set our newly-wedded prospects on.
I like it when the morning sun
makes windows slowly and moves round,
and when in lamplight it becomes a ring
of ivies, blown leaves, whisperings.
Old carpets have their share in days
remembered and forgotten, cast away.
I sing their praise, their ends and beginnings:
all worn-out, baggy, threadbare things.

AUBADE

I wake to music in the house:
one small boy playing, way below,
his fingers' trickle tickling sleep.
Another morning, and the rooms drift
back to shape and lap together
as the ship we're in
together checks its course.
Landfall of day. Another shore.
The floorboards shift; the boiler groans.
The sunlight rubs the grain
on well-loved furniture
then blazes in the brass knob on the door.

A PERSPECTIVE OF MANTEGNA

The sword swings at the soldier's hip and on
his knees the informer begs forgiveness
of the martyr, who needs must stop and bless
the man who broke a trust and brought him down
this road that leads in only one direction.
The crowd presses. They too must bear witness.
Acts they have seen before: the traitor's kiss
absolved on the way to the execution.

They all rest in the frame of the present.
Beyond the city gate, the tenement
whose windows watch the same unbending street:
betrayer and betrayed on one descent
that draws them in towards a vanishing point
where line and time and space and distance meet.

from *Clair de Lune*

TWILIGHT

The Fourteenth Earl is shivering,
in what the Americans would call his tuxedo,
at the lip of the fountain.
The moon is cold as justice, broken in lights:
his life in little white fragments,
winking leerily. The guests at the party
are guzzling, gossiping, fornicating
with reckless abandon: a dance through
the twilight of the aristocracy.
His mind fuddles. When did they start to be
this huge parody, this backdrop for a costume
binge shot lovingly in endless episodes
and financed by the fashion industry?

There was a girl once. He remembers
her white body. She laughed at him, decamped
with his money—or what was left
after the courts and the divorce, the bouts
with the vulturine attorney.
A nymph beckons. To reach her he must swim,
or wade at least. Her marble kiss
thrills through his teeth. Tomorrow the police
will halt their cars on the gravel.
The warrant will prove unnecessary: the last
of the guests will have dragged him,
sack-like, into the buttery, leaving
anonymously before the questions start.
Leaving the long wet marks on the floor and
the green shape of a man on the dew-soaked grass.

from *A Place Apart*

SUNSET

It sits on the world's edge
like Humpty Dumpty,
and its fat
tragic inevitability
puzzles them.

It doesn't fall,
it slides, slowly
under the black
horizon's rim.

They huddle together
inside his coat
and shiver and watch
the stars come out
helplessly

like all the King's men.

FORBIDDEN FRUIT

Not the garden but the tree.
Not the serpent but its voice.

Not the flower but the seed.
Not the purchase but the price.

Not the answer but the need.
Not the knowledge but the choice.

WHAT HAS COME BETWEEN THEM

What has come between them
is dumb
and unspeakable
as an idiot birth.

What has come between them
is a curl
of arrogance in a glance,
a smile's ghost.

What has come between them
is distance:
an ocean,
an arm's length.

What has come between them
ticks
like a clock
that is primed with their end.

What has come between them
is loneliness,
blank as refusal,
stupid as death.

What has come between them
is duty,
whispers,
money,
a ticket...

What has come between them
is sacrifice

pretending to be life.

MID-ATLANTIC

40° W. The sky leaden.
The steady dunk of rollers
bucking and pitching.
A limbo. And no fixed thing
to reckon progress by.
Below, boat smells:
oil and carbolic; the galley
humid, nauseous, unspeakable.
On deck, the rain and the spray
whipped back, westerly.
You pray for a clear spell,
a north-easter, a day's relief
for the spirit to settle in.
Only the engines' steady shake
is some kind of comfort.
And everywhere you are
is the point of no return.

HER LONELINESS

is as big as an iceberg

as cold, as lifeless,

a huge tear
that froze round her heart

and broke off

and now it goes drifting
away in the long winter dark.

Nine tenths is invisible.
The ten per-cent
is the meal on the table,
the story at bedtime,
her tight little laugh.

And the rest
is black as the ocean's depth

and malign, and intent
on sinking them both.

from SHEEP

I

The first of the flock
arrive in the back of Hill's waggon:
five ewes, huddling, bewildered,
loosed on a strange pasture.

A bright day, new-minted and cool,
with woolly cloud
bubbling up over the horizon—
a day for the future.

He leans on the gate,
surveys his investment.
Tilly, Meg, Barbara, Joan, Kathleen:
he names them after girls he once knew.

Today he cannot tell them apart.

II

His earliest lamb
slips into the night like a shooting star,
a yellowish sack of fingers and thumbs
that quivers to life in his hands
under the ewe's tongue.

With a midwife's tact he steps back
to admire its cries and its knock-kneed shivering.
Then he offers it down to its milky teat—
the sufficient good, the answer
to all its questioning.

In the end it will shake itself up
to its feet and stand, helpless
and leggy: a fuzzy tepee
about to collapse, to be blown flat
at the whim of the first thin wind.

When he turns from the fold
he must look back again
at this thing his touch has drawn into being,
while the lamp-light glows on his brow
where he stands—like a Christ in a painting.

from *The Odin Stone*

NEWTON'S NOTEBOOK (1667)

For 3 Prisms	0. 3. 0
For keeping Christmas	0. 5. 0
Lost at cards at twist	0. 15. 0
At ye Tavern severally	1. 0. 0

Three kings in succession
and bust again!
This season the sky's alive
and leads to the tavern—
no bed unwarmed,
the last room taken.

In the beginning
light split like a plaything
of rainbows
and I sought
something to bring it
together again.

My birthday and His
on its planetary return:
the chimney roaring
the jug half spilt,
the maid with her arms full
at the clattering door.

All this and the great
experiment
of God dividing Himself,
Logos to locus.
And the babe with his pippin cheeks
tumbled to earth.

THE UMBRELLA

The rain was the steady, soft, fine rain
of a summer day, and as she ran

from the métro, the pavements shone
and cars hissed on the black sheen

of the street. Her heels clicked and the wet
faubourg was dripping echoes—from wilted

awnings and the plane leaves on the boulevard.
Windows were steamy with breathed words

condensing there and in the puddles on shop floors.
This was the weather for *affaires*

de coeur. Her heart skipped counterpoint
against the measure of her footprint's

regular four-four, the underscore of traffic noise.
Each stride the raincoat brushed her knees.

Her breathing, too, was quick and tight,
as if anxiety constricted it.

So when she tripped the steps and pressed the bell
and saw his dark shape cross the hall,

she set her red umbrella down
on the stone flags and opened all her drowning

self to his embrace. The kiss was fierce.
He brushed the silk of wet hair from her face:

Je t'attendais—the smothered words. Then hand
in hand they turned, the door swung closed behind

them, ghostly, as they climbed the stair
like angels rising to their sphere.

As they made love, she thought of café chairs
stacked *soixante-neuf,* and he took care

to let her come and come once more
and then again, as if the mere

fact of gravity were not a law
to stop their endless spinning on love's lure.

At last their hearts' subsiding beats
grew separate; while outside, like a stray boat

drifting and unthought-of by the basement rails,
the red umbrella, upside down, sailed

on and gathered pattered droplets in.
As if that were its purpose—catching rain.

RILKE IN FLORENCE: THE HOURS

'And the hours are women
who spoil me with all kinds of
blue, shimmering delight'

Six

The earliest has the breath
of yellow roses.
She kisses me out of sleep
and she leaves me
to the luxury of warm sheets
where I dream I am
Creation stretching to become the Earth.

Seven

And I can hear the lilt
of her morning song
like water tumbling through the light
in the next room,
her long hands breaking bright
circles on the ceiling;
the basin's clink; the jug's tilt.

Eight

And this one is drying her hair
in the west wind.
She leans on the terrace rail
and lifts her face
to the sun, as a child will
to be praised,
by a world that always grants her desires.

*

Ten

Her voice is like bells
heard distantly
across the Arno, calling me.
She waits at the door
and I take her hand, carefully.
We walk together,
drawn by the churches, into their spell.

Eleven

In the darkness of the chapels
the little lights
wink at me with knowledge:
the sensuality
of the old religion. The edge
of her dress
brushes my leg and I tremble.

Twelve

As we step out into the mid-day,
the eye burns.
Her hair is spun with a nimbus
of gold-leaf.
There is too much sparkle: the grace
is invisible.
Like the face of an angel.

*

Four

Breaking the slow sleep of afternoon,
a cackling—
laughter in the street below,
like fishwives.

When I press the shutters closed
they look up,
contemptuous: I am merely a man.

Nine

In the Piazza della Repubblica,
a Gypsy band,
crossing a Balkan rhythm with a kind
of European jazz.
I would rather I had gone blind
than not seen
that vision—dancing under the first stars.

Eleven

Then dusk. Along the river streets
the lamps reflect
a postcard image of the night
on currents
running sleek and wide. So what
if I am seduced
by the glad shimmer of a prostitute?

*

RILKE IN FLORENCE: ANGELS

'My desires run riot
and out of all paintings
the angels follow me'

The masters of the *Quattrocento*
were well schooled
in gesture.
How else present
the ineffable to the ignorant?
And to paint like this
you must believe
in the body of angels.

There cannot be as many in Heaven
as here in the Uffizi,
attendant upon their offices
with the patience of centuries.

I am at ease in their company:
in mute acknowledgement
they have seemed to say
Noli me tangere
but I have felt the breath
of their wings' longing.

When God is dead
where else will they go—
unless it were
to flit behind me, unseen
in the dark corners of the world,
seeking another way
back to eternity?

RILKE IN FLORENCE: SIX FIREFLIES

'...that's what life is: six fireflies and more and more.
And you want to deny it!'

You could make a fugue
of six notes, glowing like this
on the stave of dusk,

or follow them
into a hundred byways of the wood
and watch them multiply

into infinity.
Their light's
a phosphor luminosity:

bright glimpses
through the gauze of sense
to possibility;

like casements
glinting
in the shadow-depth.

They are the city
of the stars that came to rest
a moment in this broken earth.

A DOLLS' HOUSE

Haworth

The rain shrinks us:
we pass inside dripping like pegs
from a wet washing-line.

The rooms by a miracle
are almost our size. We are
their characters, Augusta and Sneaky,

or two bad mice.
We try bonnets, a Bible
a candlestick—all miniaturised.

And the stories, the tiny stories
sewn up with the urgent fingers
of childhood's desire.

Now once upon a time there were
three dolly sisters,
their fictionalised lives,

and old granny Death who was lying close by
under one of those long black coverlets
and the gravestone sky.

BLACKCURRANT JELLY

for Jane Greening

Time has been gathering them in inky droplets,
pendant, like little studs in lobes of shade,
a bright, black buckshot, or trills of tart
quavers, dangling at random under a stave
of twigs and wires. Your fingers flit among
them like birds, the plastic tray floor pattering.
And then the scales' assay, sluicing; the long
tar-bubbling afternoon of heat, pectin,
sugar... the kitchen a Turkish bath, steamy
with fruit-sweat, the air thickening, the blood
of summer simmered through an alchemy:
the plain daylight strained into stained-glass red.
And the jar, its disc, its cellophane bonnet
nipped with a rubber band, sealed like a sonnet.

SWALLOWS

Take note of swallows
how they will make the air visible
for an instant
between the slopes of sound and light.

Observe their loops
and their rooftop jilts,
their barn-hop exits, cheating sight.

Their thought has a wing's weight
tucked in a pulse.
They are wired to the blur
of a dark door
in a map of the universe.
And because
they have come six thousand miles to ask,
we give them space.

They have slipped their time
from the spinning Earth.

Their flight is the arc of an arrow
sped to its resting-place.

BROCK

It weighs on him like a wet pelt—
the responsibility of being
an icon and a public enemy at the same time.
He knows that for centuries mankind
has been devising engines to kill him,
yet they draw him on greeting-cards,
a talisman from their tribal twilight, and revere him
like some grisly old royal while they tank up
the cyanide in the backs of their four-by-fours.
They forget that the flat macadam
is all you really need for a cull: that space
where a life he can't understand
comes flashing towards him the instant
before he enters the dark. And beyond death
he can still defy them. The crows
won't touch him. He lies like a slain god
in the verge with his prize-fighter's limbs
erect and ridiculous. He just won't stay down.
His ghost is unhappy. The only thing
that will soften his corpse is the rain.

A ROOM AT THE BACK OF THE PALACE HOTEL

You know exactly what this is:
you've walked in the frame of an Edward Hopper
where time's suspended and space is too big—
where the window's so tall that its northlight falls
at three in the afternoon like inconsolable music.
Beyond it, you know, will be emptiness: canal-wharf
and viaduct, the canyons of shadow, the featureless blocks.
Now you're shrunk in a dreamscape, a wide diorama
that waits like a stage set with armchairs and wall-lamps,
as if you're required to play with an unknown opponent
a two-handed scene, a peculiar game of emotional chess.
On the year's coldest day, the heating control
has been grounded at 'off'. Let's get out, you say.
Let's go anywhere—to the bar at least
or the wind-blent street, before the enchantment's complete,
before we are caught in a story that has no plot
and no dialogue and nothing beyond this moment
that might have existed before you conceived it
in someone's unconscious, a slight premonition
of lovers and strangers who met at a station
and drank in a café and shared information
and drifted away from the memory before it was lost.

LEAD SOLDIER

Weeding the corner of the gravel path
I dig him up, among the bony roots
of couch-grass and the sun-dried stones:
headless; footless; a victim of time's
atrocity. Somehow he is not quite
three-dimensional, but elongated,
skinny in the tatters of his uniform.
His bugler's arms are tucked, foetal,
as if he lay forever recovering.
The earth has begun to soften him
to a thin vein of mineral.
And this is the fate of soldiers—
when the hand that moved them
tires and seeks another kind of play.

RIDDLE

Grab the beast by the horns.
Wrestle it down the narrow streets
till you break its will
to skitter its own way.
Subdue it. Burden its rib-cage.
Let your children ride.
And then let it stray.
Who cares? They'll send
a herdsman to round it up
at the end of the day.

BRIDGE

What makes a bridge beautiful is its curve,
arching above an image of itself:
doubles, one sharp and one mysterious,
two versions of a tale in fact and myth.
My grandfather's is fact. The Chinese Bridge
that spans the Great Ouse at Godmanchester,
from the flat ground we call the Boys' School Hill
to the Rec, is his—it sprang from his hand.
When Brudenell's tendered for it, no-one thought
to find out if the plans from years before
were still around; my grandfather was left
to take the old bridge down and measure up,
piecing the new together on the grass
against the old bones like a giant kit.
A length of rope from pier to pier and from
the apex to the average river height
was their geometry—he and his mate,
plumbing it down to catch the arch's depth.
The distance was exactly seven feet,
with six more inches for the joints to drop,
though in the end the joints were tight and good
and didn't fall an eighth and so the bridge
flexed up six inches prouder than it should
or so one local pundit said who couldn't
himself have set a plank across a ditch.
At the official opening the Mayor
and Corporation crossed in due process
and someone made a speech and people clapped.
The men who built the bridge stood at the back.
Nobody thought a workman worth the time
to write an invitation. Fair enough:
they took a half-hour off. The plans turned up
eventually, and proved by chance the arch
was seven-feet-six above the water-top.

So there it was, perfect, exact, an arc
pure as a swan's neck, its white reflection
shifting and slipping in a weedy web.
And in the undertow the worlds invert:
In that refracted underwater land
what's yours is what your making hands have touched
and turned and worked and struggled with in thought.
One day you may look down and watch them cross:
the broken shining people in a net
of light, fragmented, lambent, as the sun
burns through an after-image of a bridge.
About their limbs the fish will glide and glint.
And who shall say whose foot is first, whose last?

from *Feast of Fools*

MAN BLOWING HIS OWN WINDMILL

Becalmed
        on his hill

he tried prayer
        but the sails
        stood like a cross
        he had to bear

He tried patience
        the millstones
        had the same idea

The ratcatcher, farmer
waggoner
        had never known
        a month so fair

Was it despair
that let him hear
        the top shaft creak?

His cheeks ballooned
        his neighbours laughed

The crows
in the cornfield
        cawed
        through the motionless air

VANITAS

her looks lie
brooding in the glassy eye

thrice in an hour
she checks and spies

no blemish
and no tell-tale sign

what we desire (she smiles)
is symmetry and youth

and she has both
(awhile) as she reflects

the mirror has two other masters:
time and truth